This Is a Let's-Read-and-Find-Out Book™

MEET THE COMPUTER

A Computer Book
1

By SEYMOUR SIMON · Illustrated by Barbara and Ed Emberley

A Harper Trophy Book · Harper & Row, Publishers

The *Let's-Read-and-Find-Out Book*™ series was originated by Dr. Franklyn M. Branley, Astronomer Emeritus and former Chairman of The American Museum-Hayden Planetarium, and was formerly co-edited by him and Dr. Roma Gans, Professor Emeritus of Childhood Education, Teachers College, Columbia University. Text and illustrations for each of the more than 100 books in the series are checked for accuracy by an expert in the relevant field. The titles available in paperback are listed below. Look for them at your local bookstore or library.

Other recent Let's-Read-and-Find-Out Book™ You Will Enjoy

A Baby Starts to Grow
Bees and Beelines
Birds at Night
Comets
Corn Is Maize
Digging Up Dinosaurs
A Drop of Blood
Ducks Don't Get Wet
Fireflies in the Night
Flash, Crash, Rumble, and Roll
Follow Your Nose
Fossils Tell of Long Ago
Hear Your Heart
High Sounds, Low Sounds

How a Seed Grows
How Many Teeth?
How to Talk to Your Computer
How You Talk
It's Nesting Time
Ladybug, Ladybug, Fly Away Home
Look at Your Eyes
Me and My Family Tree
Meet the Computer
My Five Senses
My Visit to the Dinosaurs
No Measles, No Mumps for Me
Oxygen Keeps You Alive
The Planets in Our Solar System

The Skeleton Inside You
The Sky Is Full of Stars
Spider Silk
Straight Hair, Curly Hair
A Tree Is a Plant
Water for Dinosaurs and You
Wild and Woolly Mammoths
What Happens to a Hamburger
What I Like About Toads
What Makes Day and Night
What the Moon Is Like
Why Frogs Are Wet
Your Skin and Mine

Meet the Computer
Text copyright © 1985 by Seymour Simon
Illustrations copyright © 1985 by Ed Emberley
All rights reserved. No part of this book may be used or reproduced in any manner whatsoever without written permission except in the case of brief quotations embodied in critical articles and reviews. Printed in the United States of America. For information address Thomas Y. Crowell Junior Books, 10 East 53rd Street, New York, N.Y. 10022. Published simultaneously in Canada by Fitzhenry & Whiteside Limited, Toronto.
Published in hardcover by
Thomas Y. Crowell, New York.
First Harper Trophy edition, 1985.

Library of Congress Cataloging in Publication Data
Simon, Seymour.
    Meet the computer.

    (A Harper trophy book)
    (Let's-read-and-find-out books)
    Summary: Introduces the parts of a computer and explains how they work.
    1. Computers—Juvenile literature. [1. Computers]
I. Emberley, Barbara, ill.   II. Emberley, Ed, ill.
III. Title.   IV. Series.
QA76.23.S554 1985b   001.64   84-48533
ISBN 0-06-445011-2 (pbk.)

MEET THE COMPUTER

Would you like to pilot a spaceship?
Would you like to add many numbers in a split
second? Perhaps you'd like to draw a picture and
color it in? A computer can help you do these
things and much more.

What is a computer?
And how does it work?

Let's meet the computer.
Here's one now.

It looks like a typewriter
keyboard and a TV screen.

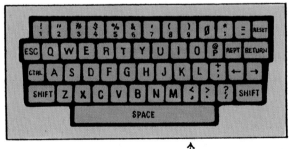

COMPUTER KEYBOARD

You turn on the power.

The screen shows a blinking dot or short line called a cursor. The cursor shows where a letter or number will appear when you press a key on the keyboard.

Press a key. The letter or number you pressed appears on the screen at the cursor. The cursor moves a short space to the right.

Whatever you type next will appear there.

The cursor keeps moving
as you type.

When you type on the keyboard, we say that you are **inputting** information. This information is often called **data** or **input**.

The computer can do different things with the input. It all depends upon what you want it to do.

If you want to play a game with a computer, you have to tell the computer how to play it. You can input a set of rules or instructions called a **program**.

A program is a list of instructions for a computer to follow.

Suppose you want to play a game called SPACE MISSION on your

computer. That means you have to input the program for SPACE MISSION so that the computer will know all about the game.

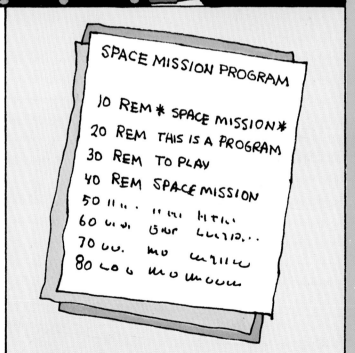

SPACE MISSION PROGRAM

10 REM * SPACE MISSION*
20 REM THIS IS A PROGRAM
30 REM TO PLAY
40 REM SPACE MISSION
50 ...
60 ...
70 ...
80 ...

CASSETTE TAPE

FLOPPY DISK

CARTRIDGE

You can input a program in an easier way than typing the whole program on the keyboard. Here's how.

The program for SPACE MISSION is stored on a cassette tape.

Programs can also be stored on "floppy disks" or on cartridges.

They store computer programs just as music is stored on records or on tape cassettes or cartridges.

When you play a record or a music tape you can hear music.

When you load a program tape into your computer you can play **SPACE MISSION** or some other game.

There are many different kinds of programs you can load into your computer. They can let you draw pictures on the screen or help you to add up numbers or do many other things.

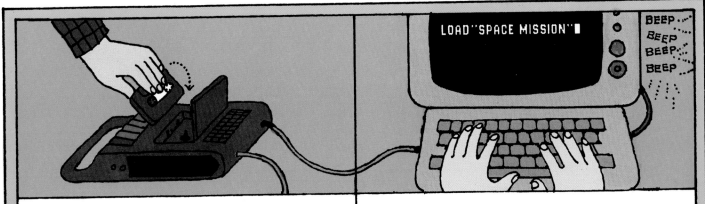

Let's load the game SPACE MISSION. You place the game tape into a cassette deck attached to the computer.

You type a command word on the keyboard that tells the computer to load the program.

The computer starts the cassette tape turning. The game program for **SPACE MISSION** is being loaded into the computer.

The game appears on the screen.

The computer uses the program instructions to play the game with you.

The invaders begin to attack!

You have to move your spaceship around on the screen.

You need a way to tell the computer which way you want your spaceship to go.

You use a joystick to input your moves.

When you move your joystick, you are giving the computer more information.

The computer **processes**
this new information.
Then the computer makes its
move. It moves the invaders
into a new position.
The computer does this
automatically, without
any help from you.

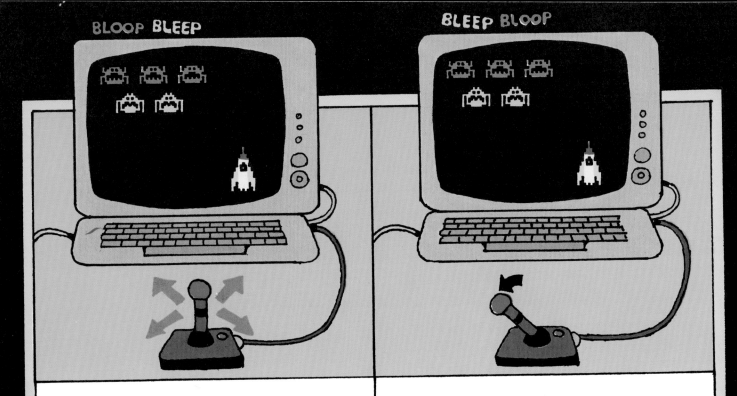

A joystick is a box with a lever that moves in all directions.

Suppose you move the joystick to the left. The direction is input to the computer. The computer now knows that you want to move the spaceship to the left.

CPU

Suppose we go inside a computer to see what really happens when you input a program and use it. Let's travel along with the information, or data, that you are inputting with your joystick.

In a split second, the input from the joystick reaches the computer's "brain." The "brain" of a computer is usually inside the keyboard. It is called a Central Processing Unit, or **CPU** for short.

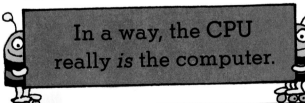

In a way, the CPU really *is* the computer.

chip

circuit

If you could look inside the CPU, you would see a tiny chip. The CPU chip is no bigger than the nail on your finger.

A CPU chip is covered with many tiny electric pathways, or circuits. Data travels along these circuits.

A chip works faster than your eye can blink. A chip can process thousands of bits of data in a second.

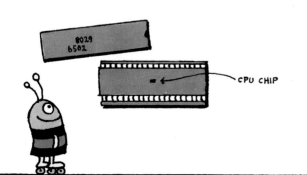

8029
6502

CPU CHIP

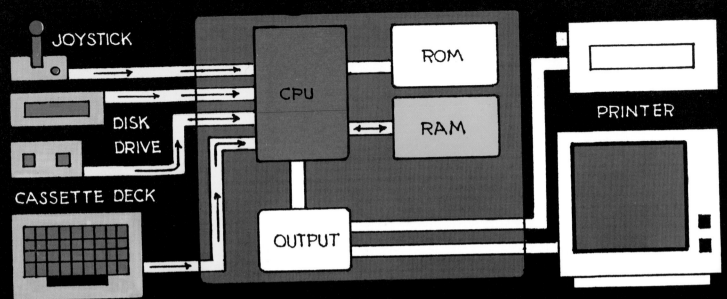

JOYSTICK

CPU

ROM

RAM

DISK DRIVE

CASSETTE DECK

OUTPUT

KEYBOARD

PRINTER

SCREEN

RAM

The CPU chip is connected to **memory** chips.

One kind of computer memory is called **RAM** (Random Access Memory).

The program information that is input from a cassette tape or a floppy disk goes to RAM.

The information you input when you type instructions on a keyboard or move your joystick also goes to RAM.

The electric circuits on a RAM chip look like thousands of little boxes.

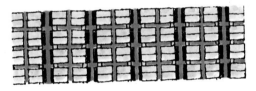

Each of the boxes is empty until information is stored in it.

Information is stored in RAM for as long as you are using the program. RAM is a kind of scratch pad, or temporary memory.

Whenever you shut off the power to the computer, all the memory is lost from RAM. The next time you switch on your computer, RAM is ready for new information.

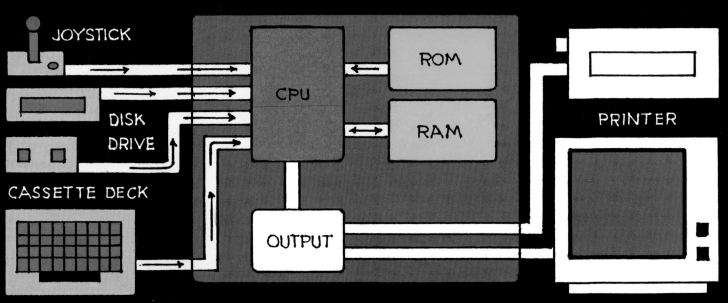

JOYSTICK

CPU

ROM

RAM

DISK DRIVE

PRINTER

CASSETTE DECK

OUTPUT

KEYBOARD

SCREEN

ROM

The computer has another kind of memory called **ROM** (Read Only Memory).

A ROM NEVER FORGETS

Unlike RAM, ROM is a permanent memory. ROM stores the information that a computer needs to follow any program you input.

Like a RAM chip a ROM chip has thousands of little boxes.

But unlike RAM, each box in ROM is always full. Each contains one little piece of information that was built in at the factory.

The information in ROM is always ready for use as soon as you turn on the computer.

A CPU needs both ROM and RAM to control the moves of invaders in a space game and to process the moves that you make with the joystick.

It also needs RAM to keep track of all the moves and how the game is going.

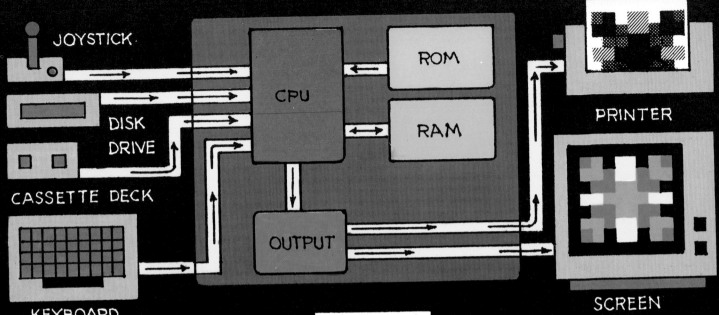

JOYSTICK

CASSETTE DECK

DISK DRIVE

KEYBOARD

CPU

ROM

RAM

OUTPUT

PRINTER

SCREEN

output

Data processing and memory storage all go on inside the computer. But no one on the outside can see what's happening.

The computer has to **output** the processed information so you can see it.

A computer has a special chip that outputs information.

OUTPUT

Suppose you are playing Animal Quiz. Let's follow the output along an electric pathway. The pathway leads from the chip out to a screen. Words and pictures appear on the screen.

We might have followed a different pathway from the computer. It would have led to a printer. A printer is like a computer's typewriter. It prints the computer's output on paper.

Now you have met the computer. You have **input** a program by loading it from a cassette tape. You have **input** information from the keyboard and a joystick.

You have visited the "brains" of the computer, its **CPU**. You have seen how a CPU chip works to **process** information.

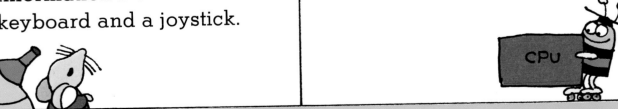

You have learned how the information you input is stored in the computer's **memory** chip called **RAM**. You have seen the **ROM** chip, which contains built-in **memory**.

Finally, you have seen how the processed data is **output** to a screen or printer.

Now when you use a real
computer at home or in school,
you will know what it is doing.

Seymour Simon was born in New York City. He received his B.A. degree from City College, New York, and did graduate work there. He was a science teacher for a number of years and now writes and edits full time.

Mr. Simon is the author of dozens of highly acclaimed science books for young readers, including HOW TO TALK TO YOUR COMPUTER; COMPUTER SENSE, COMPUTER NONSENSE; THE DINOSAUR IS THE BIGGEST ANIMAL THAT EVER LIVED AND OTHER WRONG IDEAS YOU THOUGHT WERE TRUE; HOW TO BE A SPACE SCIENTIST IN YOUR OWN HOME; and BODY SENSE, BODY NONSENSE. More than thirty of his books have been selected as Outstanding Science Trade Books for Children by the National Science Teachers Association.

He lives with his wife in Great Neck, New York.

Ed Emberley is a graduate of the Massachusetts College of Art in Boston, and a writer and illustrator of many popular children's books, including ED EMBERLEY'S DRAWING BOOK OF ANIMALS. He and his wife, Barbara Emberley, have collaborated on several books, most notably DRUMMER HOFF, winner of the 1968 Caldecott Medal. Mr. and Mrs. Emberley have illustrated other Let's-Read-and-Find-Out Science Books, including HOW TO TALK TO YOUR COMPUTER and FLASH, CRASH, RUMBLE, AND ROLL.

The Emberleys live in Massachusetts, and they sail or ski in New Hampshire in their spare time. Their children, Michael and Rebecca, have both written and illustrated children's books.